MW00533006

Scriptural Prayers for Victorious Living

Transform Your Life
Through Powerful Prayer

JAKE & KEITH PROVANCE

Scriptural Prayers for Victorious Living
ISBN 978-1-939570-49-9
Copyright © 2003, 2005, 2015 by Word and Spirit Publishing
P.O. Box 701403
Tulsa, Oklahoma 74170

Published by Word & Spirit Publishing
P.O. Box 701403
Tulsa, Oklahoma 74170

Contents

Introduction

Prayer is possibly the most captivating topic in the life of a Christian. We all know we should pray, but how often do we stop to do it, only to find ourselves at a loss for words? Sometimes we've been so busy, that talking to God feels like talking to a distant relative at a family reunion; we're not sure what exactly to talk about, and the conversation feels forced and a little bit awkward. Other times, we find ourselves overwhelmed by a major struggle with our emotions speaking so loudly that our minds can't form any words besides, "Help me." We know God has all the answers and that He can help us if He wants to. But does He want to? How do we effectively convert the way we feel—confused, nervous, or hurt—into a powerful prayer that allows God to move in our lives? This book is personally designed for such a purpose. It's filled with scriptures concerning many of the needs and hardships we all face in life to show what God truly **will** do for you. But this book goes a step further. It is filled with prayers laid out to help you communicate clearly and effectively to your loving heavenly Father. Since we've all experienced dry times when prayer just didn't come easily, we've also added Inspirational quotes by men and women of God who share a passion for the constant practice of prayer. It is our hope that their passion for prayer will take root and develop in you.

Scriptures

His compassions fail not. They are new every morning: great is they faithfulness (Lamentations 3:22-23).

This is the day which the LORD hath made; we will rejoice and be glad in it (Psalm 118:24).

In all thy ways acknowledge him, and he shall direct thy paths (Proverbs 3:6).

What shall we then say to these things? If God be for us, who can be against us? (Romans 8:31).

"God shapes the world by prayer, the more prayer there is in the world, the better the world will be, the mightier the forces against evil."

—E.M. Bounds

Start the Day Right

Lord, I thank You for the gift of this day. This is the day that You have made; I will rejoice and be glad in it. According to Your Word, Your mercy and grace are new every morning, so the sins and mistakes of my past have no place to taint the blessing of this new day.

I thank You for the wonderful gift You have provided in this day. Help me enjoy it to the fullest. Let others see You in me today, and let my words be uplifting to all those who hear them. Help me to be a blessing to the people around me and to show You honor in all that I do today.

Lord, You are bigger than any problem, any obstacle, or any calamity that lies before me so no matter what happens today, I trust You to see me through. I thank You for Your favor in every area of my life today, in Jesus' name. Amen.

Scriptures

Christ now gives us courage and confidence, so that we can come to God by faith (Ephesians 3:12 CEV).

I can do all things through Christ which strengtheneth me (Philippians 4:13).

For the LORD will be your confidence and will keep your foot from being caught (Proverbs 3:26 ESV).

❖

"I fear the prayers of John Knox more than all the assembled armies of Europe."

—Mary, Queen of Scots

Confidence

Father, I ask You to help me to be bold and confident. Let me not dwell on my shortcomings, but help me to realize that my connection with You causes me to do great things. You said in Your Word that greater is He that is in me than he that is in the world. Your Word says that I can be more than a conqueror through Christ Jesus. I can do all things through Christ who strengthens me. My confidence comes from You!

Father, I am bold to proclaim that I am confident because of Your work in me. I can operate in confidence in every area of my life, not because of who I am but because of who You are in me. Thank You, Lord, for continuing that good work which You started in me. Let Your Word bring confidence and completion in my life in Jesus' name. Amen.

Scriptures

Be on your guard; stand firm in the faith; be courageous; be strong (1 Corinthians 16:13 NIV).

Be strong and of a good courage, fear not, nor be afraid of them: for the LORD thy God, he it is that doth go with thee; he will not fail thee, nor forsake thee (Deuteronomy 31:6).

This is my command—be strong and courageous! Do not be afraid or discouraged. For the LORD your God is with you wherever you go (Joshua 1:9 NLT).

—————◈—————

"I've learned that courage is not the absence of fear, but the triumph over it."

—Nelson Mandela

Courage

Lord, help me to face the uncertainties of this life with an undaunted spirit of courage and confidence. Courage to fight for what I believe in; courage to be unshakeable in my faith; courage to have the determination never to quit or give in when times are tough.

Help me to continually remember that I can do all things through You. Even though I may feel weak or fearful at times, I know You are not. With You on my side I can overcome anything.

I draw my strength from my union with You. Help me have complete confidence in Your ability in me and through me to face any problem or overcome any difficulty. Grant me boldness that I may face any situation with firmness of purpose and a strong resolve. Through You I am more than a conqueror and a world overcomer.

Scriptures

Be careful for nothing; but in every thing by prayer and supplication with thanksgiving let your requests be made known unto God (Philippians 4:6).

If you abide in me, and my words abide in you, ask whatever you wish, and it will be done for you (John 15:7 ESV).

Therefore I say unto you, What things soever ye desire, when ye pray, believe that ye receive them, and ye shall have them (Mark 11:24).

───※───

"Let us never forget to pray. God lives. He is near. He is real. He is not only aware of us but cares for us. He is our Father. He is accessible to all who will seek him."

—Gordon B. Hinckley

Developing a Lifestyle of Prayer

Father, You said that through prayer I should let my requests be made known to You. Your Word says that whatsoever things I desire when I pray, when I believe that I receive them, I shall have them. I ask and desire for prayer to become so significant to me that it becomes my natural response to every situation in life.

Help me to not let the busyness of life rob me from the joy, privilege, and power of spending time with You. Put a desire in my heart to pray more throughout my day, knowing that time spent in prayer is really time spent talking to a dear Friend and loving Father. Show me how to establish certain times of the day to pray and let me not be distracted during my prayer time.

In Jesus' name I pray. Amen.

Scriptures

If any of you lack wisdom, let him ask of God, that giveth to all men liberally, and upbraideth not; and it shall be given him (James 1:5).

The steps of a good man are ordered by the LORD: and he delighteth in his way (Psalm 37:23).

Teach me good judgment and knowledge: for I have believed thy commandments (Psalm 119:66).

"Is prayer your steering wheel or your spare tire?"

—Corrie ten Boom

Discernment

Lord, I ask You for discernment. Give me wisdom and insight concerning all the matters in my life. Help me to be sensitive to Your voice. Give me direction and guidance concerning every decision that I am faced with today. Help me to have a discerning heart and mind when I deal with people and issues that must be confronted. Bring clarity to my heart and mind regarding any situation that requires my attention and help me to respond with the appropriate action.

Help me to make decisions objectively and not emotionally. Allow me to see with Your eyes and hear with Your ears and operate in Your wisdom so that I make the right choices in my life. Help me to determine Your will concerning every area of my life.

As I acknowledge and worship You, I thank You that You direct my steps and order my life by Your Spirit. In Jesus name I pray, amen.

Scriptures

The LORD will keep you from all harm—he will watch over your life (Psalm 121:7 NIV).

There shall no evil befall thee, neither shall any plague come nigh thy dwelling (Psalm 91:10).

Yea, though I walk through the valley of the shadow of death, I will fear no evil: for thou art with me; thy rod and thy staff they comfort me (Psalm 23:4).

"Safety comes in our nearness to God, not in our distance from our enemies."

—Dillon Burroughs

Divine Protection

Dear heavenly Father, I pray for divine protection. I know that You said in Your Word that You would never leave me nor forsake me. I believe that Your angels go before me to protect me and keep me from harm and danger of any kind.

Lord, Your Word says that You hide me under Your wings, that no evil shall befall me, and that no plague or calamity shall come near my home.

I pray for safety over our home and my vehicles. Wherever I go and whatever I do, I thank You that I operate in Your divine protection. I pray for safety on the highways. I ask that You protect my residence from burglaries and vandalism. I pray that You protect me from any threats of physical, mental, or emotional violence.

Father, I pray for Your peace that passes all understanding to guard my heart and mind. Thank You for Your protection in every area of my life. In Jesus' name, amen.

Scriptures

So then faith cometh by hearing, and hearing by the word of God (Romans 10:17).

Now without faith it is impossible to please God, for the one who draws near to Him must believe that He exists and rewards those who seek Him (Hebrews 11:6 HCSB).

Faith is the confidence that what we hope for will actually happen; it gives us assurance about things we cannot see (Hebrews 11:1 NLT).

"Could it be that God intends for us to
have the same kind of audacious faith—
the kind of faith that dares to believe God
for the impossible—as a normal way of life?"

—Steven Furtick

Faith

Lord, I thank You that You have given every believer a measure of faith. Give me understanding of how faith works and how I can apply it in my life. Lord Jesus bring maturity and perfection to the faith that You have placed within my heart. Impart to me insight and wisdom concerning how to have daring faith.

You said that faith comes by hearing the Word of God. I make a conscious decision to read and listen to Your Word, so my faith can grow. You said that without faith it is impossible to please You. Faith is the assurance and confirmation—my title deed—of things that I hope for and the proof of things I do not see. I thank You, Lord, that the faith that is in my heart perceives the unseen promise as a real fact.

Faith is alive and working in my life. By faith, I receive all that You have done for me. In Jesus' name, amen.

Scriptures

A faithful man shall abound with blessings (Proverbs 28:20).

Let us hold fast the confession of our hope without wavering, for he who promised is faithful (Hebrews 10:23 ESV).

His lord said unto him, Well done, good and faithful servant; thou hast been faithful over a few things, I will make thee ruler over many things: enter thou into the joy of thy lord (Matthew 25:23).

——◆——

"Prayer is not overcoming God's reluctance.
It is laying hold of His willingness."

—Martin Luther

Faithfulness

Father, I ask You to help me be faithful in every area of my life. Help me to have dedicated loyalty to those for whom I work, to my family and friends, and to my church.

But most of all, Lord, help me to be faithful to You. Help me to endure any hardship like a soldier, knowing that I'm working for You and not for any man or woman. Let my faithfulness and obedience to You be untainted by a heart of unwillingness. Help me to stay strong and resist the temptation to be offended because of what others say or do. Help me to take control over my emotions and not let how I feel dictate how I act..

Help me to live my life so that at the end of my days I will be ushered into Your presence with the words, "Welcome, thou good and faithful servant."

In Jesus' name I pray. Amen.

Scriptures

For his anger lasts only a moment, but his favor lasts a lifetime; weeping may stay for the night, but rejoicing comes in the morning (Psalm 30:5 NIV).

For surely, O LORD, you bless the righteous; you surround them with your favor as with a shield (Psalm 5:12 NIV).

For the LORD God is a sun and shield; the LORD bestows favor and honor; no good thing does he withhold from those whose walk is blameless (Psalm 84:11 NIV).

※

"When you accept the fact that your true identity includes being an overcomer, you will never settle for less than a miracle."

—Craig Groeschel

Favor

Lord, I ask that Your favor surround me like a shield. Wherever I go and whatever I do, I thank You for being such a good God. I ask that my life would be evidence of your goodness. Let Your favor flow through every area of my life, producing supernatural increase. Thank You for favor in all my affairs, favor that opens doors of opportunity and favor that influences all I come into contact with in a great way.

Lord, I ask that You would develop my expectancy for favor in my everyday life. Help me to not be satisfied with less when You have called me to live a life of abundance. Lord, I don't want to have small thinking or small living. I want Your blessings and favor to be so rich in my life that not only am I blessed, but I'm able to bless all those around me.

Thank You, Lord, for favor in Jesus' name. Amen.

Scriptures

"Bring the whole tithe into the store-house, that there may be food in my house. Test me in this," says the LORD Almighty, "and see if I will not throw open the flood-gates of heaven and pour out so much blessing that there will not be room enough for it" (Malachi 3:10 NIV).

Every man according as he purposeth in his heart, so let him give; not grudgingly, or of necessity: for God loveth a cheerful giver (2 Corinthians 9:7).

Give, and it will be given to you. A good measure, pressed down, shaken together and running over, will be poured into your lap. For with the measure you use, it will be measured to you (Luke 6:38 NIV).

---

*"God will either give you what you ask,
or something far better."*

—Robert Murray McCheyne

Finances

Dear Father, I know that it is Your will to bless me. I know that as I am faithful to pay my tithes and give to Your work, You will bless me. You said that as I give it shall be given back to me, good measure, pressed down, and shaken together.

Debt has no place in my life. I ask that You would help me pay back everything I owe.

Reveal to me how to use discretion in my spending habits. Help me to be practical, sensible, and intelligent in all my buying decisions.

Give me creative ideas and new insight to create income. Help me be productive and diligent in my job. Give me favor with my employer.

I thank You, Lord, that increase and promotion come from You. Show me how to be financially successful so that I can be an abundant giver to Your work and a blessing to others. In Jesus' name I pray. Amen.

Scriptures

He canceled the record of the charges against us and took it away by nailing it to the cross (Colossians 2:14 NLT).

Even if we feel guilty, God is greater than our feelings, and he knows everything. Dear friends, if we don't feel guilty, we can come to God with bold confidence (1 John 3:20-21 NLT).

Brethren, I count not myself to have apprehended: but this one thing I do, forgetting those things which are behind, and reaching forth unto those things which are before, I press toward the mark for the prize of the high calling of God in Christ Jesus (Philippians 3:13-14).

—❧—

"Prayer breaks all bars, dissolves all chains,
opens all prisons, and widens all straits
by which God's saints have been held."

—E.M. Bounds

Forgiveness

Father, in Jesus' name I give You all the hurt and bitterness in my life. I refuse to carry the burden of those past hurts in my heart anymore. I ask for Your forgiveness in my life. It's hard to come to You because of all the guilt and regret I feel. I know you want me to be free from this burden. Let your forgiveness develop in me to the point where I can rid myself of regret and shame. And Lord, because You have been so forgiving to me, I ask that You give me the strength to forgive others in the same way You forgive me.

Help me to not harbor bitterness toward anyone. Help me forgive and forget so I can be completely free in every way. I will not let the pain of my past rob me of the promise of my future. Thank You, Lord, for freeing me from my past. In Jesus' name I pray. Amen.

Scriptures

O give thanks unto the LORD; for he is good; for his mercy endureth for ever (1 Chronicles 16:34).

Do not be anxious about anything, but in everything by prayer and supplication with thanksgiving let your requests be made known to God (Philippians 4:6 ESV).

Be thankful in all circumstances, for this is God's will for you who belong to Christ Jesus (1 Thessalonians 5:18 NLT).

"I have come to believe that the prayer of praise is the highest form of communication with God, and one that always releases a great deal of power into our lives."

—Merlin R. Carothers

Giving Thanks

I want to thank You for Your Word that You gave us. Through Your Word, I have the wonderful opportunity to read Your thoughts and get to know Your heart. Your Word is such a precious gift. Every word frees and uplifts me. Thank You for honoring me with it.

Thank You for the gift of the Holy Spirit, my ultimate guide and comforter. Knowing Your Spirit is always with me, fills my heart with security and thanksgiving.

Thank You for Your inexhaustible supply of forgiveness and love. No matter how many times I have messed up, You are still there with open arms to welcome me back.

You are truly a friend who sticks closer than a brother. You are always there to take care of my every need. Help me to never take for granted all that You have done for me. In Jesus' name I pray, amen.

Scriptures

Little children, you are from God and have overcome them, for he who is in you is greater than he who is in the world (1 John 4:4 ESV).

I have told you these things, so that in Me you may have [perfect] peace. In the world you have tribulation *and* distress *and* suffering, but be courageous [be confident, be undaunted, be filled with joy]; I have overcome the world. [My conquest is accomplished, My victory abiding] (John 16:33 AMP).

But if the Spirit of him that raised up Jesus from the dead dwell in you, he that raised up Christ from the dead shall also quicken your mortal bodies by his Spirit that dwellth in you (Romans 8:11).

"God honors bold prayers, because bold prayers honor God."

—Mark Batterson

The Greater One in Me

I thank You, Lord, that greater is He that is in me than he that is in the world. You are within me, energizing, motivating, empowering, and equipping me for total victory today. Because You reside in me, Satan and all the forces of darkness are no match for me. Sin, sickness, and lack don't stand a chance. You are greater than any circumstance I might face. You are greater than any obstacle that comes up before me. You are greater than any challenge that comes into my life. You are greater than any adversity that comes against me. Lord, You are greater than my own doubts, insecurities, or uncertainties.

I am more than a conqueror through You. I can face the circumstances of life with boldness and confidence in You. You are greater, and You live in me. You put me over; You cause me to succeed; with You, in Jesus' name, I cannot be overcome, I cannot be defeated, and I cannot fail!

Scriptures

The LORD directs the steps of the godly. He delights in every detail of their lives (Psalm 37:23 NLT).

Trust in the LORD with all thine heart; and lean not unto thine own understanding. In all thy ways acknowledge him, and he shall direct thy paths (Proverbs 3:5-6).

The LORD says, "I will guide you along the best pathway for your life. I will advise you and watch over you (Psalm 32:8 NLT).

<hr>

"We never now how God will answer our prayers, but we can expect that He will get us involved in His plan for the answer."

—Corrie ten Boom

Guidance

Heavenly Father, I ask you for guidance and direction concerning Your plan and purposes for my life, for those who are led by the Spirit of God are the sons of God. Help me to be keen to hear and quick to obey the voice of Your Spirit. Reveal to me Your perfect will regarding the decisions that I need to make. Let not money, relationships, or advice of any kind be the determining factor in the decisions I make in my life. Help me to exercise wisdom and utilize these things, but not allow them to be the ultimate reason for making any decision. Help me not lean on my own understanding but trust the voice of Your Spirit.

I thank You, Lord, that by the wisdom of Your Word and the guidance of Your Spirit, I can navigate my way through any circumstance. Help me to be sensitive to the guidance of the Holy Spirit. In Jesus' name I pray. Amen.

Scriptures

But he was wounded for our transgressions, he was bruised for our iniquities: the chastisement of our peace was upon him; and with his stripes we are healed (Isaiah 53:5).

He that spared not his own Son, but delivered him up for us all, how shall he not with him also freely give us all things? (Romans 8:32).

He sent his word, and healed them, and delivered them from their destructions (Psalm 107:20).

———◆———

"Whatever you ask me in prayer,
you will receive, if you have faith in me."

—God (Matt. 21:22 Ref.)

Healing

Dear heavenly Father, I come before You for healing in my body. I ask for Your healing power to touch my body right now. Help me to be strong in my faith to receive Your healing for my body.

Jesus took stripes on His back for my healing; He bore my sickness and carried my diseases. The Bible says He himself took our pains in His own body and that with His stripes we were healed.

I receive the promise of the Scriptures regarding my healing. Jesus paid the price for my healing so that I am made whole. Now, Lord, I receive Your Word and believe it. I thank You and praise You for the healing that has begun in my body. Whether I feel any change in my body or not, I know that Your healing power is at work within me at this very moment. Thank You, Lord, for my healing! In Jesus' name I pray, amen.

Scriptures

The name of the LORD is a strong tower; the righteous run to it and are safe (Proverbs 18:10 NIV).

But the Lord is my refuge; my God is the rock of my protection (Psalm 94:22 HCSB).

But me? It's good for me to be near God. I have taken my refuge in you, my Lord God, so I can talk all about your works! (Psalm 73:28 CEB).

⋘⋙

"Be strong and of good courage; be not frightened, neither be dismayed; for I am your God and I am with you whenever you go."

—God (Joshua 1:9 ref)

The Lord Is My Refuge

Lord, You are my refuge and strong tower. You are my fortress and place of security and safety. Help me to live in that place of confidence and peace.

Because I have made You my refuge and my dwelling place, no evil shall befall me; no plague or calamity shall come near my home or my family. You give Your angels charge over me to preserve me in all my ways. Wherever I go and whatever I do, Your angels protect me from harm, injury, and evil.

Though I may walk in the midst of peril, it will have no effect on me. Because You have set Your love on me, You will deliver me and set me on high. Your mercy, grace, and kindness surround me like a shield. You will be with me in times of trouble, and You will deliver me and honor me. With a long life, You satisfy me and show me Your salvation. In Jesus' name. amen.

Scriptures

But let patience have her perfect work, that ye may be perfect and entire, wanting nothing (James 1:4).

And we know that all things work together for good to them that love God, to them who are the called according to his purpose (Romans 8:28).

But the fruit of the Spirit [the result of His presence within us] is love [unselfish concern for others], joy, [inner] peace, **patience [not the ability to wait, but how we act while waiting]**, kindness, goodness, faithfulness, gentleness, self-control (Galatians 5:22-23 AMP).

———◆———

"Whenever I have prayed earnestly, I have been heard and have obtained more than I prayed for. God sometimes delays, but He always comes."

—Martin Luther

Patience

Dear heavenly Father, I pray for patience in my life. Help me to trust You and to know that You have everything under control. When life is hectic, demanding, and busy, show me how to not let frustration and anxiety steal patience out of my heart.

Allow me, Lord, to trust the work that You are doing in me. Lord, help me to run the race that is before me with patience, not to run too fast or strive to make things happen in my future, but to let Your will be worked out in my life.

Help me to be patient in prayer. When it seems as if You are not answering my prayers as quickly as I desire, help me to patiently trust in Your timing.

I know change and challenges are a normal part of life. I ask for Your help to be patient during those times of tests and trials.

In Jesus' name I pray. Amen.

Scriptures

The LORD is my rock, and my fortress, and my deliverer; my God, my strength, in whom I will trust; my buckler, and the horn of my salvation, and my high tower (Psalm 18:2).

We have conducted ourselves with godly sincerity and pure motives in the world, and especially toward you. This is why we are confident, and our conscience confirms this. We didn't act with human wisdom but we relied on the grace of God (2 Corinthians 1:12 CEB).

People with their minds set on you, you keep completely whole, Steady on their feet, because they keep at it and don't quit. Depend on God and keep at it because in the Lord God you have a sure thing (Isaiah 26:3-4 MSG).

⋘━━━⋙

"I have been driven many times upon my knees by the overwhelming conviction that I had nowhere else to go. My own wisdom and that of all about me seemed insufficient for that day."

—Abraham Lincoln

Relying on God

Lord, I thank You that I can rely on You in all things. Give me clear instruction and keep me firmly planted on the unchangeable truth and strong foundation that is Your Word. I rely on and trust in Your Word and promises. Enlighten me with Your understanding concerning the plan You have for my life. Set me free from all hindrances. Make me secure and capable in You. Help me to maintain a steadfast resistance to the attacks of the enemy, and live in a place of blessing and prominence because of Your love for me.

Help me to see that Your Spirit is forever with me, helping me and guiding me. He is my dear ally and closest friend. He gives me wisdom, insight, and clarity concerning the decisions I make. Through Your Word, Your faithfulness and promises are established in my heart and bring strength and stability to my life. In Jesus' name I pray, amen.

Scriptures

Am I now trying to win the approval of men, or of God? Or am I trying to please men? If I were still trying to please men, I would not be a servant of Christ (Galatians 1:10 NIV).

The fear of man bringeth a snare: but whoso putteth his trust in the LORD shall be safe (Proverbs 29:25).

But just as we have been approved by God to be entrusted with the gospel, so we speak, not to please man, but to please God who tests our hearts (1 Thessalonians 2:4 ESV).

"Why don't you start believing that no matter what you have or haven't done, that your best days are still out in front of you."

—Joel Osteen

Rejection

Lord, help me to not base my joy or happiness on what others think about me. Let me not be discouraged or become emotionally distraught because of a suffered wrong. Heal my heart and fill me with Your joy and peace. Remind me who I am to You, what I have because of You, and what I can do because You are within me.

Let me not be resentful or offended by others, no matter what they may say or do to me. I will not retaliate, gossip, or hold a grudge against them. But I cast the care of this situation over on You. I will not speak evil of them. I refuse to be bitter or angry.

Let these thoughts and feelings stop here and now before they grow into discouragement or hate. I thank You, Lord, that You will never leave me or forsake me. I'm happy to call You my best friend and strong ally in life. In Jesus' name, amen.

Scriptures

And do not be conformed to this world [any longer with its superficial values and customs], but be transformed *and* progressively changed [as you mature spiritually] by the renewing of your mind [focusing on godly values and ethical attitudes], so that you may prove [for yourselves] what the will of God is, that which is good and acceptable and perfect [in His plan and purpose for you] (Romans 12:2 AMP).

Casting down imaginations, and every high thing that exalteth itself against the knowledge of God, and bringing into captivity every thought to the obedience of Christ (2 Corinthians 10:5).

***

"Every Christian needs a half-hour
of prayer each day, except when
he is busy, then he needs an hour."

—Francis de Sales

Renewing My Mind

Dear heavenly Father, it is my desire to keep my mind pure and clear from anything that would hurt me or damage my relationship with You.

You said in Your Word to take every thought captive. Yet sometimes I feel as if my thoughts have held me captive. Thoughts of worry, fear, regret, and lust have no right to plague my mind any longer. I choose to think about good things, Lord. When I am tempted, help me overcome the attacks on my mind with answers from Your Word. Lord, let me be quick to respond to wrong thoughts and desires by replacing them with proper thoughts.

I make a quality decision to meditate on Your Word and to keep my mind pure and receptive to Your voice. Lord, I know that with Your help, I can win the battle in my mind and overcome every wrong thought with the power of the spoken Word. In Jesus' name I pray. Amen.

Scriptures

Therefore if any man be in Christ, he is a new creature: old things are passed away; behold, all things are become new (2 Corinthians 5:17).

He refreshes *and* restores my soul (life); He leads me in the paths of righteousness for His name's sake (Psalm 23:3 AMP).

Restore unto me the joy of thy salvation; and uphold me with thy free spirit (Psalm 51:12 NIV).

"When God forgives, He at once restores."

—Theodore Epp

Restoration

Lord, You are the great Redeemer. You have redeemed my life from destruction. You have restored my soul, and You have forgiven me of my past failures. You have given me a new lease on life. You are an awesome God. I praise and exalt You.

You have replaced my mourning with joy. You have taken away my heavy burden and filled my heart with thanksgiving. You have taken the shame of my past and given me a blessed and exciting hope for the future.

You, Lord, have restored me. You have given me a purpose in life, a divine calling. I thank You for it and for placing Your favor upon my life so that I might accomplish Your purpose with gladness.

Let Your miracle working restoration power be continually at work within every area of my life. But don't let it stop there. Let it overflow out of me so that all may see just how good You are! In Jesus', amen.

Scriptures

Therefore if any man be in Christ, he is a new creature: old things are passed away; behold, all things are become new (2 Corinthians 5:17).

But if the Spirit of him that raised up Jesus from the dead dwell in you, he that raised up Christ from the dead shall also quicken your mortal bodies by his Spirit that dwelleth in you (Romans 8:11).

Jesus told her, "I am the resurrection and the life. Anyone who believes in me will live, even after dying (John 11:25 NLT).

"Praying in faith is not denying that you have problems, but believing that God is bigger than your problems."

—Dr. Jerry Fowler

Resurrection Power

Lord, I thank You that I am not controlled by my flesh or the natural desires of my old nature. The old man is dead, and a new man is living inside of me. The same Spirit that raised my Lord Jesus from the dead dwells within me. The same resurrection power gives life, health, and vitality to my mortal body.

Your resurrection power in me renews my soul and strengthens my spirit. By Your power in me, Lord, I can do all things. That power gives me boldness and confidence to be a witness for You. Your power is working in me, changing me into Your image and developing in me Your nature.

By the same resurrection power, my life has taken on a new dimension—a dimension of overcoming faith, spiritual perseverance, and total and complete victory in every area. Thank You, Lord! In Jesus' name, amen.

Scriptures

So here's what I want you to do, God helping you: Take your everyday, ordinary life—your sleeping, eating, going-to-work, and walking-around life—and place it before God as an offering. Embracing what God does for you is the best thing you can do for him (Romans 12:1 MSG).

Study *and* do your best to present yourself to God approved, a workman [tested by trial] who has no reason to be ashamed, accurately handling *and* skillfully teaching the word of truth (2 Timothy 2:15 AMP).

Show me thy ways, O Lord; teach me thy paths (Psalm 25:4).

"Those blessings are sweetest that are won with prayer and worn with thanks."

—Thomas Goodwin

Spiritual Growth

Lord, help me to grow spiritually. Help me to not let my daily activities and responsibilities fill my life to the point that I have no time for prayer, worship, and devotional times with You.

Father, please prompt me to spend time with You. Help me remember to put You first, blocking out time every day to invest in my spiritual growth. Give me the strength to say no before I over-commit or take on more than I can handle.

Lord, increase my desire for spiritual things. Reveal to me areas where I need to grow. Help me to be conscious of everyday opportunities to pray, to meditate on Your Word, to speak Your Word, and to apply Your Word to my life. I humble myself before You. Teach me Your ways, direct my steps, let Your Word become alive in me. Help me to always be sensitive to what You want to do in my life. In Jesus' name I pray. Amen.

Scriptures

What? know ye not that your body is the temple of the Holy Ghost which is in you, which ye have of God, and ye are not your own? (1 Corinthians 6:19).

I beseech you therefore, brethren, by the mercies of God, that ye present your bodies a living sacrifice, holy, acceptable unto God, which is your reasonable service (Romans 12:1).

Don't assume that you know it all. Run to God! Run from evil! Your body will glow with health, your very bones will vibrate with life! (Proverbs 3:7-8 MSG).

"We have to pray with our eyes on God, not on the difficulties."

—Oswald Chambers

Staying Physically Fit

Lord, I understand that my body is the temple of the Holy Spirit. You told me in Your Word to present my body as a living sacrifice, holy and pleasing to You. I want to respect and please You by being fit for duty. I recognize that if I am overweight and out of shape, it will affect my ability to serve my family, my friends, and the work of the Gospel.

Help me choose the eating and exercise program that is best for me. Help me to make conscious lifestyle choices that will cause my body to function in health and vitality. Give me determination and courage to say no to health-destroying foods and substances. Show me how to incorporate a daily exercise routine into my schedule, and help me to discipline myself to follow that plan.

I rejoice in the results I will see as I exercise and subject myself to You. In Jesus' name I pray. Amen.

Scriptures

He giveth power to the faint; and to them that have no might he increaseth strength (Isaiah 40:29).

But they that wait upon the LORD shall renew their strength; they shall mount up with wings as eagles; they shall run, and not be weary; and they shall walk, and not faint (Isaiah 40:31).

I can do all things [which He has called me to do] through Him who strengthens *and* empowers me [to fulfill His purpose—I am self-sufficient in Christ's sufficiency; I am ready for anything and equal to anything through Him who infuses me with inner strength and confident peace] (Philippians 4:13 AMP).

———

"To get nations back on their feet, we must first get down on our knees."

—Billy Graham

Strength

Father God, I ask you to give me strength. Impart to me courage, fortitude, and determined resolve. May I never become worn out in doing what's right. Let the power of the Holy Spirit undergird me, lift me up and infuse me with your strength.

Lord, I know that many are the afflictions of the righteous, but You will deliver me out of them all. Help me stay strong in my faith as I wait upon Your deliverance. Help me stay strong when others doubt me. Help me stay strong in the face of anything and everything that dares to confront me, a child of the Living God!

When the odds are stacked against me, when trouble is all around me, when fear and fatigue are biting at my heels, I will stand my ground knowing that ultimate victory is certain in You! In Jesus' name, amen.

Scriptures

Peace I leave with you, my peace I give unto you: not as the world giveth, give I unto you. Let not your heart be troubled, neither let it be afraid (John 14:27).

Come unto me, all ye that labour and are heavy laden, and I will give you rest (Matthew 11:28).

If you work the words into your life, you are like a smart carpenter who dug deep and laid the foundation of his house on bedrock. When the river burst its banks and crashed against the house, nothing could shake it; it was built to last (Luke 6:48 MSG).

"Every day I pray, I yield myself to God, the tension and anxieties go out of me and peace and power go in."

—Dale Carnagie

Stress

Lord, help me to live free from stress. Fill me with Your peace. Show me how to trust You and be calm, even when the circumstances of my life are screaming so loudly that it's difficult to hear anything else. Let me rise above turmoil and agitation to a place of perfect peace in Your presence.

By faith, and in obedience to your Word, I cast all my cares, all my anxieties and all my stress on You. I receive Your peace in exchange. Help me to focus on You and Your Word and not allow stress to affect my life in any way. Show me how to develop a calm spirit and the spiritual strength to not let the cares of this world cause frustration or pressure in my life.

I choose to worship You and praise You. I purpose to have a grateful heart, no matter what I am going through. With Your help and guidance, I am confident that I can live a stress-free life.

Scriptures

Haven't I commanded you: be strong and courageous? Do not be afraid or discouraged, for the Lord your God is with you wherever you go (Joshua 1:9 HCSB).

Now thanks be unto God, which always causeth us to triumph in Christ, and maketh manifest the savour of his knowledge by us in every place (2 Corinthians 2:14).

In conclusion, be strong in the Lord [draw your strength from Him and be empowered through your union with Him] and in the power of His [boundless] might (Ephesians 6:10 AMP).

❈

"He who kneels the most, stands the best."

—D. L. Moody

Strong in the Lord

Lord, I ask You to give me strength. Help me draw strength from You so that the demands of daily living won't pull me down or wear me out. Let Your strength produce spiritual resilience, physical stamina, and mental sharpness in me.

Help me resist the temptation to give in or give up. For when my strength begins to waver, Yours will take over. Help me draw strength from You so I will not grow weary. You are my source of energy and my source of strength.

In Your presence I find strength to endure, power to overcome, and sustaining joy to conquer any challenge that may come my way. As I study and meditate on Your Word, I thank You that I find comfort and peace and my strength is renewed.

Scriptures

I will praise thee; for I am fearfully and wonderfully made: marvellous are thy works; and that my soul knoweth right well (Psalm 139:14).

But let it be [the inner beauty of] the hidden person of the heart, with the imperishable quality *and* unfading charm of a gentle and peaceful spirit, [one that is calm and self-controlled, not overanxious, but serene and spiritually mature] which is very precious in the sight of God (1 Peter 3:4 AMP).

Even before he made the world, God loved us and chose us in Christ to be holy and without fault in his eyes (Ephesians 1:4 NLT).

"Prayer is the rope that pulls God
and man together. But, it doesn't pull
God down to us; it pulls us up to him."

—Billy Graham

Valuing Myself

Heavenly Father, help me to see myself the way You see me. You gave me gifts and talents that are specific and unique to me so that I can accomplish great things on this earth. Help me to discover them more fully.

You placed a value on my life when You sent Your sinless, spotless Son to come to this earth and die the death that I should have died. You gave the life of Your own Son just so I could be free. Your love and admiration for me is unfathomable and sometimes so hard to see when I look at how imperfect I am. So have mercy on me in those moments. Even when I mess up big and repeatedly, I ask that You would remind me who I am and what You paid for me. Help me to realize that, even with all my shortcomings, You still believe in me. Help me to do the same for myself. In Jesus' name, amen.

Scriptures

In all thy ways acknowledge him, and he shall direct thy paths (Proverbs 3:6).

I have it all planned out—plans to take care of you, not abandon you, plans to give you the future you hope for (Jeremiah 29:11 MSG).

If you don't know what you're doing, pray to the Father. He loves to help. You'll get his help, and won't be condescended to when you ask for it. Ask boldly, believingly, without a second thought (James 1:5-6 MSG)

"Prayer lays hold of God's plan and
becomes the link between His will and
its accomplishment on earth."

—Elisabeth Elliot

Walking in the Fullness of God's Plan

Lord, in all my ways I recognize, acknowledge, and honor You. I put You first in my life. I lean on You, trust in You, and am confident in You, Lord. Grant me Your insight and understanding regarding every area of my life. Because I acknowledge You, regardless of what others say, how I feel or what uncertainties lie before me, I know that You direct, make straight, and regulate all my ways. My steps are sure, and my path is clear. My future is bright and promising.

Fulfill Your plans and purposes for my life. Use me, Lord, to make a difference in this world.

Let my life be a testimony of Your grace, love, and mercy. Let me be so full of You that there is none left of me. Consume my life, Lord, to the point that others only see You in me. In Jesus' name I pray. Amen.

Scriptures

So do not fear, for I am with you; do not be dismayed, for I am your God. I will strengthen you and help you; I will uphold you with my righteous right hand (Isaiah 41:10 NIV).

The LORD is my light and my salvation; whom shall I fear? the LORD is the strength of my life; of whom shall I be afraid? (Psalm 27:1).

For God hath not given us the spirit of fear; but of power, and of love, and of a sound mind (2 Timothy 1:7).

"The wise man in the storm prays
God not for safety from danger
but for deliverance from fear."

—Ralph Waldo Emerson

When You Are Battling Fear

Dear Father, You have told me to not fear because You are with me. You uphold me, and You sustain me. Your Word says that though I walk through the valley of the shadow of death, I will fear no evil, because you are my Shepherd and Protector.

I will not be afraid of bad news, bad situations, or bad outcomes because You are my rock, my fortress, and my deliverer. You give me the strength and courage to handle any situation. You have promised that You will never leave me nor forsake me.

Your Word says that You have not given me a spirit of fear, but instead You gave me power, love, and a sound mind. I will consider Your Word above the fear that tries to overtake me. When I am tempted to fear, I will look to You. In You, Lord, I am strong and fearless. In Jesus' name I pray. Amen.

Scriptures

Is anyone crying for help? GOD is listening, ready to rescue you. If your heart is broken, you'll find GOD right there; if you're kicked in the gut, he'll help you catch your breath. Disciples so often get into trouble; still, GOD is there every time (Psalm 34:17-19 MSG).

I know how to get along and live humbly [in difficult times], and I also know how to enjoy abundance *and* live in prosperity. In any and every circumstance I have learned the secret [of facing life], whether well-fed or going hungry, whether having an abundance or being in need. I can do all things [which He has called me to do] through Him who strengthens *and* empowers me [to fulfill His purpose—I am self-sufficient in Christ's sufficiency; I am ready for anything and equal to anything through Him who infuses me with inner strength and confident peace] (Philippians 4:12-13 AMP).

"Prayer will get you out of a pinch, prayer will get you out of a crisis, prayer will get you out of your dilemma, prayer will get you out of your trouble."

—TD Jakes

When You Are Facing a Crisis

Lord, help me to realize that life is full of the unexpected. I desire to not become fearful, anxious, or overwhelmed in this present situation. Help me to not react in confusion, worry, or desperation, but instead, replace those thoughts and emotions with Your Word and a good attitude.

Help me keep my mind fixed on You and the power of Your Word. Give me wisdom and insight concerning any decisions I need to make or actions I need to take to do my part in resolving this crisis.

I count it all joy when I am faced with challenges and problems, knowing that the trying of my faith builds my patience and godly character. You have promised to be with me and see me through this crisis. Give me courage, strength, and fortitude to not give up or give in but to patiently keep trusting You until I can stand triumphantly over this situation! In Jesus' name, amen.

Scriptures

"If you'll hold on to me for dear life," says God, "I'll get you out of any trouble. I'll give you the best of care if you'll only get to know and trust me. Call me and I'll answer, be at your side in bad times; I'll rescue you, then throw you a party. I'll give you a long life, give you a long drink of salvation!" (Psalm 91:14-16 MSG).

I have told you all this so that you may have peace in me. Here on earth you will have many trials and sorrows. But take heart, because I have overcome the world (John 16:33 NLT).

Peace I leave with you; My peace I give to you; not as the world gives do I give to you. Do not let your heart be troubled, nor let it be fearful (John 14:27 NASB).

"We can be tired, weary and emotionally distraught, but after spending time alone with God, we find that He injects into our bodies energy, power, and strength."

—Charles F. Stanley

When You Are Feeling Discouragement

Lord, I pray that You would help me overcome this discouragement. I ask for Your help, Lord. These discouraging thoughts weigh heavy on me. I know it is not Your will for me to feel and think this way.

Help me replace my fears with faith, my doubts with belief, my worries with trust, and my cowardice with courage. Lord, help me focus on You and not on my problems.

I know that there is no problem too big, no hurt too deep, no mistake so bad that You cannot heal my hurt and restore my confidence. Help me trust You and cast my cares, anxiety, and worries upon You.

I believe in You, Lord, and I know that You will see me through. Give me endurance and determination to not give up, cave in, or quit. I refuse to allow discouragement to control my life. In Jesus' name I pray, amen.

Scriptures

I will strengthen the weary and renew those who are weak (Jeremiah 31:25 CEB).

Who satisfieth thy mouth with good things; so that thy youth is renewed like the eagle's (Psalm 103:5).

And let us not be weary in well doing: for in due season we shall reap, if we faint not (Galatians 6:9).

"No one is a firmer believer in the power of prayer than the devil; not that he practices it, but he suffers from it."

—Guy H. King

When You Are Fighting off Fatigue

Lord, I ask You for strength in my body. Restore to me energy and vitality to go on. I understand that mental frustrations and worries can bring on weariness and tiredness, so I cast every care in my life over onto You. I ask You to strengthen my spirit, soul, and body today. I draw from Your encouragement and the power of Your Word. Renew my strength, Lord.

Help me, Lord, to not become weak, weary, or faint in doing what's right. Let Your joy fill my heart and strengthen my body.

Thank You for Your peace and rest. Help me do what is right for my body. Help me to properly rest, exercise, and eat so I am not fighting against my body but helping to keep my body strong. I pray, Lord, that my youth would be renewed as the eagle's.

In Jesus' name I pray. Amen.

Scriptures

If any of you lack wisdom, let him ask of God, that giveth to all men liberally, and upbraideth not; and it shall be given him (James 1:5).

But the wisdom from above is first pure [morally and spiritually undefiled], then peace-loving [courteous, considerate], gentle, reasonable [and willing to listen], full of compassion and good fruits. It is unwavering, without [self-righteous] hypocrisy [and self-serving guile] (James 3:17 AMP).

Therefore see that you walk carefully [living life with honor, purpose, and courage; shunning those who tolerate and enable evil], not as the unwise, but as wise [sensible, intelligent, discerning people] (Ephesians 5:15 AMP).

———❖———

*"As you walk in God's divine wisdom,
you will surely begin to see a greater measure
of victory and good success in your life."*

—Joseph Prince

Wisdom

Father, I come before You asking for Your wisdom. You said in Your Word that if anyone lacks wisdom, he could ask of You and You would give to him liberally. Lord, give me wisdom concerning my relationships, as well as guidance and direction to properly manage my responsibilities.

Lord, show me how to operate in wisdom and understanding in every area of my life. No matter how small the task, I ask for Your wisdom to guide me. Before I undertake any new projects or consider any purchases, let Your wisdom teach me how to properly manage my time and resources.

Help me not be easily swayed or convinced by emotionalism or by pressure from others; instead, I thank You for common sense, guidance, and discernment functioning and flowing in my life. I thank You that by wisdom my house is established and that I have discretion in all my activities. In Jesus' name, amen.

Scriptures

Don't fret or worry me. Instead of worrying, pray. Let petitions and praises shape your worries into prayers, letting God know your concerns. Before you know it, a sense of God's wholeness, everything coming together for good, will come and settle you down. It's wonderful what happens when Christ displaces worry at the center of your life (Philippians 4:6-7 MSG).

Cast thy burden upon the LORD, and he shall sustain thee: he shall never suffer the righteous to be moved (Psalm 55:22).

What shall we then say to these things? If God be for us, who can be against us? (Romans 8:31).

"The more you pray, the less you'll panic.
The more you worship, the less you worry.
You'll feel more patient and less pressured."

—Rick Warren

Worry

Lord, reveal to me how to live my life free from worry. I know that worrying can take over my thought life if I'm not careful. Your Word says that all things work together for good to those who love You. I recognize that I can't do anything to change my circumstances by worrying, except to make them worse. Lord, I don't want to walk through life wondering and worrying that something bad might happen. Help me have victory over this. Help me put my trust in You, regardless of what happens or doesn't happen. I know You are a good God and You will work it out. Whatever I need, You've got it. Help me really grasp that truth so I can truly be free from worry.

I Thank You that I am free from worry, and I have victory in Jesus' name. Amen.

Scriptures

When thou liest down, thou shalt not be afraid: yea, thou shalt lie down, and thy sleep shall be sweet (Proverbs 3:24).

I will lie down and sleep in peace, for you alone, O LORD, make me dwell in safety (Psalm 4:8 NIV).

It is vain for you to rise up early to sit up late, to eat the bread of sorrows; for so he giveth his beloved sleep (Psalms 127:2).

"Any concern too small to be turned into a prayer is too small to be made into a burden."

—Corrie ten Boom

End the Day Strong

Lord, as I come to You at the end of this day, I thank You for being faithful to me. Thank You for your provision. Thank You for sustaining and protecting me. Thank You for Your blessings in every area of my life.

Heavenly Father, forgive me of anything that I may have said or done that was displeasing to You. If I offended anyone, I ask You to forgive me and to heal the hurts I have caused.

Now help me to not worry or have any frustration or anxiety about any thing that happened today. I cast all the cares and concerns of today's events upon You. Help me to forget the past and look toward tomorrow. I thank You that no matter how many times I stumbled today, I can start fresh and new in You tomorrow. I thank You for a restful night's sleep, in Jesus' name. Amen.

NOW AVAILABLE

VOLUME 2

KEEP
CALM
AND
TRUST
GOD

JAKE PROVANCE & KEITH PROVANCE

TOPICS INCLUDE . . . HOPE, LOVE, STRENGTH, PEACE, COURAGE, CASTING YOUR CARES, FACING A CRISIS, PRESS ON, FORGIVENESS, AND JOY